Original title:
Life: More Questions Than Answers

Copyright © 2025 Creative Arts Management OÜ
All rights reserved.

Author: Derek Caldwell
ISBN HARDBACK: 978-1-80566-204-4
PAPERBACK: 978-1-80566-499-4

Mirrors Reflecting Questions

Why do socks disappear in the wash?
Is it a portal to sock-topia?
Do cats think we're just weird?
Or is it us that's the enigma?

What's up with chicken crossing roads?
Is there a chicken conspiracy?
Do you ever wonder about shoes?
Can they dream of fancy feet?

Ephemeral Certainties

Why do we forget where we parked?
Is my car playing hide-and-seek?
Do we really need all these keys?
Or just a magic unlocker?

Why do we bake cakes with holes?
Is it to keep us on our toes?
Can dessert be a serious thing?
Or just a slice of pure joy?

Treading the Unknown

What if my plants have a life chat?
Do they gossip when I'm not there?
Do I speak fluent whale with my fish?
Or do they think I'm quite the catch?

Why do we fear what we don't know?
Is it just the thrill of surprise?
Do we dodge shadows in the night?
Or just want to meet the moon?

Clouds of Speculation

Are clouds just cotton candy up high?
Do they crave a scoop of ice cream?
What if rain is just a tear?
Of a cloud that watched a sad dream?

Why do birds seem to laugh at us?
Did they just get the best joke ever?
Do they plan their trips with flair?
Or do they think we're as clever?

Cracks in the Facade

In a room full of mirrors, do I see my best side?
Or have I just hidden where my doubts like to slide?
With a smile like a mask, I dance with delight,
While the cracks wear a grin that keeps me up at night.

I sprout a good story, hopes high in the air,
But the punchline is missing, as if it's not there.
Jokes tumble in chaos, like socks on the floor,
While sanity chuckles, then races for the door.

Beyond the Veil of Certainty

Questions float like balloons drifting sky-high,
Pop! goes the answer, it just passed me by.
I chase it with hope wrapped in ribbons of doubt,
But the truth plays a game, and I'm left out.

I searched for the guide in a book and a song,
Yet wisdom is clueless; it hums along wrong.
With a wink and a nudge, it dances plain air,
While I'm left in the lurch, trying hard not to care.

Reflections in the Dark

What's hiding in shadows? Is it fear or a snack?
I squint at the mirror but the answer won't crack.
With each twist and turn, I ponder the plot,
Do I find out the truth, or simply just not?

The darkness arms giggles, like a sneaky old friend,
As I tumble through riddles with nowhere to spend.
Laughter bounces off walls, a riddle-filled spree,
While I laugh at my questions like they're all just for me.

The Wisp of an Answer

I caught a glimpse once of a thought in a breeze,
It teased me with silence, then made my head freeze.
Like a wisp of cotton candy, sweet but unsure,
It crumbled to nothing; I'm left craving more.

With a cheer and a jig, I keep chasing that spark,
But that phantom of reason just giggles in dark.
So I'll clutch at the echoes, the whispers untrue,
And craft my own answers from the nonsense I rue.

Seekers of the Unseen

We wander through the starlit void,
With thoughts that dance like a jolly lloyd.
Where did the socks all disappear?
And why does cheese always taste like fear?

With questions bouncing like a ball,
Is that a shadow or a wall?
We chuckle at what we do not know,
As mysteries sprout like weeds that grow.

In the cupboard, are ghosts our peers?
Or do they just hang out after beers?
We scratch our heads with puzzled faces,
As knowledge hides in hidden places.

So raise a toast to the unseen clowns,
Who dance around our faded towns.
With giggles swirling like autumn's breeze,
We sip on questions like fine affinities.

Riddles in the Twilight

In twilight's glow, we ponder deep,
Are dreams just tricks? Or secrets we keep?
Why are there always socks mispaired?
And why's the remote always so ensnared?

The sun dips low, a crafty grin,
Do ants play chess when we're not in?
What's up with cats and their strange stares?
Are they plotting while we brush our hairs?

Questions swirl like leaves in flight,
Is being silly truly wrong or right?
We chase the riddles through the night,
Amidst the giggles, our spirits ignite.

Unanswered Echoes

Echoes bounce in a chamber vast,
Why can't we remember the day that passed?
Where did I leave my car keys again?
And why do I laugh at my own old pen?

Questions drift like bubbles in air,
Why does cereal always go everywhere?
Do fish ever get thirsty? Or just chill?
As laughter sneaks up with stealthy thrill.

We ask and smile, perplexed and sweet,
Why do all my shoes have holey feet?
The echoes ring with a comical cheer,
As we wander through what feels unclear.

The Maze of Moments

In the maze of moments, we twist and turn,
Searching for answers that never return.
Why does chocolate melt, but not on my shirt?
And why is my dog always covered in dirt?

We laugh at the quirkiness all around,
Why do birds hop and yet never bound?
Is a nut just a seed in disguise?
Or is it merely a trick of the eyes?

Questions flit like butterflies bright,
As we dance through the fun of the night.
Embrace the nonsense, let thoughts ignite,
For in all the chaos, there's sheer delight.

Echoes of the Unexplained

Why are socks always lost?
The laundry's a black hole, I'm almost cost.
Do clouds have feelings? Do they sigh?
When it rains, do they just get shy?

What hides behind the fridge door?
A gathering of dust bunnies, or maybe more?
Do fish ever get bored of swimming around?
Or do they gossip of treasure yet to be found?

Is my cat plotting to take over the house?
Or simply waiting for me to drown in my louse?
Why do we park on driveways, so absurd?
Then we drive on parkways—who made that word?

Do chairs ever feel lonely when empty?
And do books judge readers—could they be petty?
Why does Monday always seem so mean?
It must be secretly plotting to intervene.

Riddles in the Silence

Why do we yawn when we're not tired?
Are we just trying to get the world wired?
Do bugs sit and ponder life's big plot?
Or are they just wondering where they forgot?

What's the point of elastic bands?
Do they dream of future rubber bands?
Is cereal soup? The debate is bold!
Or are noodles just pasta, I'm told?

If a sneeze is a mini explosion,
Is a giggle a laugh's smooth motion?
Why do we press harder on the remote?
When the channel change feels like a boat?

Do clouds ever see, just like we do?
Do they talk politics or choose a brew?
In the end, are we all just questions?
Floating in humor, beyond our obsessions.

In Search of Elusive Truths

Is cereal breakfast or just all day?
Why do we eat it in a bowl, I must say?
Do pancakes feel pride when stacked up high?
Or do they get dizzy, saying goodbye?

When did adults forget how to swing?
Was it the coffee, or just work's sting?
Do shoes know when they will be worn?
Or do they yearn for a sock's cute adorn?

Why is the fridge such a wonderland?
With leftovers that defy where we stand?
Do mirrors laugh when we preen too much?
Or do they just mock with a gentle touch?

Can a rainbow taste like cotton candy?
Or is my imagination just too handy?
In this twisted maze of thoughts we roam,
We giggle, we ponder, and still call it home.

The Art of Questioning

Do you think a goldfish ever forgets?
Or is their memory like a series of bets?
Why do we call it 'fast food' with glee?
When waiting in line feels like eternity?

Do shoes ever wish they could just walk?
Or are they content just listening to talk?
Can a phone feel shunned when it's not in use?
Or does it love the peace, enjoying a snooze?

What's the reason behind the question mark?
Is it uncertain, or just a tiny spark?
Why does the TV ask if we want to upgrade?
As if it knows the fun that we made?

When did turning off the lights mean sleep?
Is it a sign of dreams that we keep?
In this circus of thoughts that swirl and glide,
The questions keep coming, our curious guide.

Labyrinth of Dreams

In a maze of thoughts, I roam,
Chasing shadows, far from home.
Why do socks disappear in the wash?
Is there a hook where they all slosh?

Questions swirl like autumn leaves,
Tangled thoughts that no one believes.
What's the secret to a happy cat?
Do they ponder, or just sit flat?

Each night's dream, a puzzle made,
A wild circus parade unafraid.
Why do I run but never flee?
Is my brain playing tricks on me?

So here I squint at the starlit sky,
Sure of nothing, but wondering why.
If I find the exit, will I dance?
Or stay exploring, lost in chance?

Continual Questions

Why is the pizza so much better,
When it's served with a side of cheddar?
What's the proper way to eat a pie?
Is it fork, or spoon, or do we just try?

Who decided that grass is for shoes?
Made out of leather, or canvas hues?
If time is money, where's my cash?
Did I spend it all on things that crash?

Round and round, like a rolling dice,
Why do I stumble, yet think I'm precise?
Is there a manual for dating?
Or just a sign that says: keep hating?

With every logo and brand I see,
Why is confusion analogous to glee?
If answers hid beneath my bed,
Would I dare open the box instead?

Portraits of Unknowing

A canvas stretched, with colors bright,
But every brushstroke feels just slight.
What captures joy in a single frame?
Can laughter fit? Or is that just lame?

I paint a scene of clashing dreams,
With unicorns and rainbow beams.
Why does the cat give me that look?
Am I a page in a curious book?

A selfie snapped, but what's the goal?
Is it the smile, or the soul?
If I pose in front of the moon,
Will it sing me a soft, sweet tune?

Each stroke a mystery, a quirky dance,
Hoping each twist gives life a chance.
In this gallery where questions play,
Is ignorance bliss? Maybe, I say!

Where Certainty Fades

The solid ground begins to shake,
What's real, what's fake? Oh, for goodness' sake!
Why do puddles dance in the street?
Are they practicing, or just feeling the beat?

Behind closed doors, I hear a creak,
Is it a ghost, or just a leak?
When clocks have no hands, do they still tick?
What's the magic behind the trick?

Doubt spreads like a wild white paint,
Am I a sinner, or merely quaint?
Does the sun shine just to tease?
Or does it ponder, like gentle breeze?

In the corners where shadows play,
Questions bloom like flowers in May.
As certainty fades, I dance in the light,
Waltzing with questions, oh what a sight!

Between Here and There

Am I awake or lost in dreams?
The coffee's cold, or so it seems.
I trip on thoughts, they fly away,
Why does it feel like yesterday?

Do ducks know the way to the park?
They quack profound under the dark.
I wave at clouds that look so gray,
Is it just me, or is it a play?

Do socks hide when I'm in a rush?
Or do they laugh, and then just hush?
The cat's got wisdom like a sage,
Yet I can't find a single page.

Between here and there, what's my fate?
Is it too late to grab a plate?
With questions buzzing like a bee,
Maybe it's simpler just to be.

Starlit Questions

Why do stars twinkle at night?
Is the moon just a giant light?
Are aliens watching my bad dance?
Or did I simply miss my chance?

If time travels, where did it go?
Did it stop by for a game of throw?
Are socks and spoons in on the plot?
Is this really all that I've got?

Do fish ever dream of flying high?
Or stare at the waves and wonder why?
Are we all just puzzles, mixed and matched?
With riddles in corners, scratched and hatched?

As constellations flicker, I muse,
Got questions galore, but bless my snooze.
With starlit giggles, I start to grin,
Maybe the answers lie deep within.

A Canvas of Unanswered Dreams

Why is my toaster a rebel soul?
It burns my toast, like it's on a roll.
Do crayons know the colors of fate?
Or do they just sit and contemplate?

If wishes come true, why stay in bed?
Why not ride a unicorn instead?
Do cupcakes dream of frosting on top?
Or do they just long for a sweet shop?

Are clouds jealous of birds in the sky?
Do they wonder how they can fly high?
If questions were paint, what would they be?
Just splashes of humor, wild and free?

In this canvas, absurd yet bright,
I dance with the echoes of day and night.
With every question, a brushstroke there,
Who needs the answers? I like the flair.

Threads of Ambivalence

Is it wrong to eat cake for breakfast?
Or right to lounge in a silly dress?
Do goldfish plot their great escape?
Or are they simply glue on a tape?

What happens to socks at the laundromat?
Do they form a club? Imagine that!
Are birds just taxis in the blue?
Or do they wonder if we're quite askew?

If I whisper secrets to my fridge,
Does it giggle, or just play bridge?
Do clocks mock me as I run late?
Or do they simply take a break?

In threads of doubt, I stitch my seams,
Mixing up laughter with fanciful dreams.
For each silly question that dances my way,
I shrug and grin; it's all fair play.

The Unfolding Enigma

In shadows where the questions play,
I ponder things I lose each day.
Like socks that vanish in the wash,
Are they off to some grand frosh?

The clock ticks loud, yet time moves slow,
Do fish have thoughts? I'd like to know!
As ducks parade in silly rows,
Their quacks might hide their deep inner woes.

The cat stares back, a masterful gaze,
In its mind, perhaps a thousand ways.
Do we all just chase our tails?
Or write our stories in the gales?

With every chuckle, I glide through doubt,
Is the meaning lost, or just about?
In laughter lies the puzzle, true;
The riddle's joy is waiting for you.

Footprints in a Fog

Wandering through a misty haze,
I trip on thoughts in quirky ways.
Are sandwiches meant for the shy?
Or do they secretly wish to fly?

Fog hides the path, I don't know where,
But that's okay; I brought a chair!
In every step, a question blooms,
Like why do cat videos light up rooms?

A ghostly figure walks along,
It's just my shadow, singing a song.
What is the sound of one leaf clapping?
Or is that only my brain napping?

Lost in the fog, I twirl around,
Chasing laughs that can't be found.
In this dense mist, I carry on,
Collecting giggles 'til the dawn.

Navigating Through Ambiguity

I set sail on a sea of doubts,
With questions swirling, round about.
Do clouds ever get tired of drifting?
Or is it the sunshine they keep lifting?

My compass spins with hope and fear,
It points to snacks, so bring them here!
Is the treasure buried deep in thought?
Or is it snacks that can be bought?

Navigating waves of what could be,
Do trees have secrets, boughs set free?
An octopus raises a single hand,
To wave goodbye to the dry land.

In this swell, I dance and ask,
For answers hidden beneath the flask.
With each laugh, I steer my way,
Through the foggy doubts of the day.

Where Fates Intertwine

In a café of dreams we sip our tea,
Do we know where they'll take us to be?
The sugar stirs with questions on fire,
Did the spoon just tap out a choir?

With strangers dropping hints like crumbs,
I ponder if thoughts can make us dumb.
Do raindrops play chess on window panes?
Or do they gossip about our pains?

Fates entwined, like pasta in sauce,
Who knew that art could be such a boss?
Is my shoe on the right or left?
Or just a plot twist, in quest bereft?

In laughter's spark, I find my way,
To knit together this funny display.
With questions in hand, let's toast the night,
To whimsical wonders, oh what a sight!

Questions in the Wind

Why's a cloud so white and fluffy?
Do they all enjoy being puffy?
If trees could talk, what would they say?
Probably just 'leaf me alone' all day.

Do ants ever get tired of marching?
Or are they in a parade, just arching?
Are stars jealous of the sun's hot fame?
Or do they simply play a twinkling game?

If fish could fly, where would they go?
To visit the clouds and put on a show?
Can rainbows swim, or do they just float?
What would they wear if they had a coat?

Why do we trip over what we don't see?
Is there a committee that sets us all free?
Questions in wind, swirling about,
Laughter and pondering, never a drought.

Echoes from the Deep

Is that a whale or just my stomach?
Echoes in the ocean, isn't it comic?
Fish look at me with curious eyes,
Do they think I'm the ultimate surprise?

Why don't dolphins ever play cards?
Do they fear a loss, or life with guards?
When crabs dance sideways, what's in their head?
Maybe they wonder about dreams in bed.

Do seagulls giggle when they steal a fry?
Is it a feast or a bad pie in the sky?
Mermaids, if real, would they brush their hair?
Or trade it for bubbles without a care?

Echoes deep in the watery blue,
Questions are plenty, as we paddle through.
With laughter and foam, we float on our way,
Wondering what other nonsense might sway.

Fragments of Understanding

What's the sound of one sock in the wash?
Does it miss its partner, or is it posh?
Does a pencil ever wish it could write?
Or just sit in silence, feeling contrite?

Can a hamster run farther than a car?
If you ask it nicely, will it take you far?
When toast lands butter-side down, oh dear!
Is it fate or just breakfast that we fear?

Do moose ever ponder why they're so tall?
Or if they should wear shoes, do they stall?
Do keys feel lonely when they're left behind?
Or are they just happy, being unconfined?

Besides, who really likes to fold socks?
A question with fragments that totally rocks!
Yet in every giggle and pondering glance,
We find bits of truth in the silliest dance.

The Great Inquisition

Why's an onion the center of tears?
Is it their way of playing on fears?
Are cats secretly plotting their reign?
Or just napping all day, free from any pain?

If gravity takes a holiday, what then?
Will we float like balloons in our den?
Do chairs ever cry if no one's around?
Or do they just wait, firm and unbound?

Why do we scribble down all our thoughts?
Is it to communicate with our pots?
Can an umbrella be sad in the rain?
Or does it just dance, never feeling pain?

The great inquisition plagues our hearts,
With riddles and giggles, it stubbornly starts.
In every question, funny or wise,
We unwrap new layers, the mind's own surprise.

Shadows Cast by Questions

Why's the sky so blue, so wide?
Is it just paint the clouds collide?
Do trees gossip in the breeze?
Or is that just my mind at ease?

Do fish swim slower when they dream?
And do sandwiches really scream?
When cats think, what do they ponder?
Are we all just fish in a pond, I wonder?

Do socks have a secret life at night?
Or do they just plot their next flight?
Is time really just a funny game?
Or are we all just stuck in a frame?

Why do humans chase their tails?
Is it because reason fails?
Do bananas ever feel confused?
Or have they simply been amused?

Whispers of Uncertainty

Do birds ever plan a heist?
Or is worm-hunting just their main slice?
Is coffee just liquid motivation?
Or a brew for dreams and contemplation?

When did crayons first get a name?
Did they ever play the color game?
Do we live in a giant dome?
Or is 'home' just a tricky poem?

Why do muffins have tops so round?
Is that where the magic is found?
Are clocks in a hurry just for show?
Or do they secretly want to glow?

Are trees plotting our escape?
While we're stuck in our daily shape?
Do shadows laugh at our expense?
Or just sit back, enjoying suspense?

The Puzzle of Existence

Do puzzles ever miss their pieces?
Or is it just their mind that ceases?
Is the moon a giant cookie?
Or just a rock that's feeling spooky?

Why do we ask but never know?
Is truth a plant that will not grow?
Do jellybeans have a master plan?
Or did they just create 'Candyland'?

Why do we laugh and sometimes weep?
Is joy just a secret we keep?
Do giraffes reach for dreams so high?
Or do they just paint the sky?

When did evening start to sigh?
Does it have answers, oh my oh my?
Are we just riddles wrapped in rhyme?
Or funny stories lost in time?

Shadows of Doubt

Why do shoes always run away?
Do they dream of holiday?
Do goldfish hold deep discussions?
Or just float in their aquatic cushions?

Do clouds ever feel lonely at night?
Or do they just drift in delight?
Are there unicorns lost in the fray?
Or are they just hiding away?

When does toast become too burnt?
Is it when the butter's spurned?
Can your phone really hear your thoughts?
Or does it just see the weird spots?

Are we all just figments of dreams?
Or is normal just how crazy seems?
Do pancakes flip in a frenzy?
Or have they all become too friendly?

What Lies Beneath?

Beneath the surface, things can hide,
Like socks that vanish, or cats that ride.
Where do they go? Is there a clue?
The answers dance like morning dew.

Secrets linger in the air,
Like why do ducks not seem to care?
Do fish get bored in water's embrace?
And why can't I find my phone in this place?

Jellybeans fall from the sky at night,
But only when you've lost the light.
Are they real, or just a dream?
Oh, what a wacky scheme!

Pondering puzzles, oh what a bore,
Like why my keys are never on the floor.
What's under the bed, or in the fridge?
Maybe it's time to build a bridge.

Fleeting Whispers

Whispers float like dandelion seeds,
Carrying worries and funny needs.
Why can't I find where my other sock went?
Maybe it's plotting, in a world it invents.

Donuts are round, but where's their hole?
Is it hiding like my last piece of coal?
Questions swirl like leaves in the breeze,
Life's little quirks can bring us to tease.

A cat with sunglasses is lounging fast,
Wondering why time never lasts.
Do fish dream of swimming in the air?
Or have they too, a riddle to share?

Laughter tickles like a feather's light touch,
When you trip on nothing, oh, isn't it such?
With giggles abound, we twirl and spin,
Embracing the nonsense tucked beneath our skin.

The Search for Meaning

Looking for meaning in the tea leaves,
Did the cat spill it? Oh, who believes?
Is it in a cookie, or perhaps a pie?
Maybe it's found in a double-fried fry.

Questions stack up like pancakes high,
Like why does my jacket fly when I sigh?
Do birds gather round for gossip to share?
Or is that just a product of clean air?

Mirrors reflect the oddest sights,
Like me in pajamas at midnight flights.
Are we merely puppets on a string?
Or stars in a sitcom, ready to swing?

The quest seems endless, much like my socks,
Every drawer filled, and still confusion knocks.
But amidst the chaos and humorous plight,
We laugh and we wonder well into the night.

Quandaries of the Heart

Where does love spring from, a river or sea?
Is it chocolate dipped, or just plain glee?
Can it dance on the tip of a pencil so small?
Or bounce like a ball at the next big hall?

Heartstrings tug, an invisible dance,
But also draw us into a trance.
Why do we swoon at silly old puns?
And reason with chocolate? Oh, isn't it fun?

Mismatched socks and wandering thoughts,
Are quirks of the heart, like fanciful knots.
Can a giggle break down every wall?
Or does it just echo, through the hall?

In this comedy, we play our parts,
With questions and laughter, we fill our carts.
So here's to the journey, the fun and the play,
As we dance with our doubts, day after day.

Trails of Inquiry

Why does toast always land down?
Is gravity a bit of a clown?
Why do socks disappear in the wash?
Or do they just run off in a rush?

Why do cats stare at the wall?
Are they having a secret ball?
Do birds know all the latest jokes?
Or do they just play silly folks?

Why do we sing in the shower?
Is the shampoo singing power?
Why do we trip on the same old ground?
Is it just us or are the rocks all round?

Why does coffee taste better in mug?
Is there a magic in every hug?
Questions float like bubbles in air,
And leave us chuckling everywhere!

Unraveling the Unseen

Why do we park on driveways, you say?
And then we drive on the parkway, hooray!
Where do all the pens go to play?
They vanish like magic every day.

Why is it called a building, so grand?
When it's already built, isn't that planned?
How come when we slow down to gaze,
Time speeds up like it's in a race?

Why do we push harder on the remote?
Like it's got a secret little note?
Do ducks have a secret society?
Quacking about their own variety?

Where does the day go when it's done?
Does it roll over just for fun?
Questions whirl like leaves in the breeze,
Tickling our brains, like playful tease!

A Canvas of Unanswered Whys

What's with all the keys on our rings?
They jingle like it's a band that sings.
Why do we find coins in the couch?
Is there a treasure map we should slouch?

Why do we order a 'meat pie'?
When it's just a fancied up slice of sky?
How do we lose track of our thoughts?
Are they playing hide and seek, madly fought?

Why do we always look for our phone?
While talking to someone on our own?
Do shoes really need to match so much?
Can't they just have a little fun and such?

What happened to those Caramello bears?
Are they enjoying life up the stairs?
Questions flow like paint on a wall,
A canvas of giggles, standing tall!

The Weight of Wondering

Why do ducks make such a fuss?
In their world, is it all a plus?
Why does pizza always taste great?
Is the cheese pulling a secret date?

Why does ice cream melt so fast?
Like it's racing with time to outlast?
Do plants really dance when we're not near?
Is it a party that only they cheer?

Why are we always losing our keys?
Why can't they just hang out in the breeze?
Is there a ghost in the blender's deep?
Whipping up chaos while we sleep?

What's the deal with an eight-legged freak?
Is it just a really shy cheek?
Questions tumble like marbles on floors,
Bringing laughter into all the chores!

Hues of the Uncertain

Why does toast always land buttered down?
Is it fate? Or just a feathery clown?
When socks go missing, where do they flee?
Can they party like it's a sock jubilee?

Curious minds twist like pretzel shapes,
Are fruit flies just failed escapees?
If cats can land on feet, why not pillows?
Who knew they were such daring fellows?

The fridge hums trivia, ever so sly,
Knows all the secrets of the leftovers pie.
A cabbage can tell you of cabbage-y woes,
Yet, it just sits while nobody knows.

From birthdays to socks, it's all a grand show,
Questions abound, like a wild rodeo.
But laugh we must, for the answers stay shy,
Embrace the bizarre, let curiosity fly!

Steps into the Abyss

What's the sound of one shoe dropping?
And why do remote controls keep swapping?
Do goldfish practice their swim squad turns?
Or do they simply swim and munch on ferns?

They say the grass is greener, is it true?
Or does it just hide from the morning dew?
If a tree falls and no one is there,
Does it whisper secrets? An unsung affair?

Coffee stains on paper, marks of a dream,
Does the universe plot while we all scheme?
If socks were leaders, would they wear a crown?
Or just lounge about, half-heartedly brown?

In this dance with the curious night,
Each question a flicker, a clumsy light.
Wiggle and jive, let confusion be fun,
For we all know the answers just run!

The Spectrum of Inquiry

Why do we park on driveways, you say?
Shouldn't it be a parkway where we play?
If laughter can cure what ails you tonight,
Then why do comedians always take flight?

Is water wet, or does it just float?
Do fish wear blankets? For warmth they gloat?
If the moon's made of cheese, what of the sun?
A pizza in space is too big for fun!

Why do we call it a building, you ask?
When it's built already, that's quite the task!
Do cookies crumble to share a good hope?
Or just to spread crumbs— a sweet little trope?

With questions galore in this circus we play,
Each chuckle a spark in the matter we weigh.
So let's hold our hands up, and give them a wave,
As we traverse the whims of the curious brave!

Chronicles of Confusion

If a cow jumps over, what's the big deal?
Does it crave popcorn, or is it surreal?
Why do we echo the sounds of a beep?
Is it just a warning, or do phones need sleep?

Is it a good idea to follow a duck?
Or will it lead us into swirling bad luck?
When is a door not a door, I propose?
When it's ajar, right? But who really knows?

We ponder the stars while sipping on tea,
What do ants think of when they disagree?
If socks are indeed magical garb,
Do they plot together a world with no barb?

With giggles and questions, we frolic along,
In this zany mix-up, we all belong.
So let's raise a glass to the things left unclear,
For confusion is sweet, and it brings us good cheer!

The Sound of Questions

Why does toast always land jam-side down?
And why do cats always wear a frown?
If socks disappear, where do they go?
Is it the dryer, or just a sock-throw?

Do fish ever get thirsty, it's hard to tell?
And why does chocolate make me feel swell?
If Mondays had a flavor, what would it be?
A bitter surprise with no guarantee?

Why do we yawn, is it contagious too?
And why can't I remember what I just knew?
If the chicken crossed, where'd it roam?
To find the egg or just head home?

Why do we laugh, is it just for fun?
Or do we chuckle at life's strange run?
In all of the chaos, one thing is clear,
The questions we ask bring us cheer!

Flickering Light of Understanding

Why do we park on driveways, I ponder this Toad?
While the street's a real jumble, a traffic abode.
Is the sky really blue, or just playing pretend?
Does it change like our moods, or is that just the trend?

If a sneeze comes with a 'bless you,' what's its cost?
Are the germs just as friendly, or have they been lost?
Do we count our blessings or just check our phones?
Is wisdom just nonsense wrapped up in tones?

Do clouds take vacations or just float and stare?
And why do they seem to hang heavy in air?
If I eat my greens, will I grow really tall?
Or will I just bounce like a rubber ball?

What's the secret to socks never finding a pair?
Do they dance in the closet or plot with a flair?
In the flickering dark, we stumble and sway,
Finding humor in questions that brighten the gray!

Navigating the Unknown

Why does the map always lead us astray?
When corners are turned to find a new way?
Are we meant to wander with no place to go?
Or is that where the best stories grow?

If ducks get to quack, why don't we try?
Is it a bird thing, or do we just shy?
When you step on gum, is it fate's cruel dare?
Or just a sticky trap with no warning to share?

Do shoes really wear down on just one side?
Or is it my style that I cannot abide?
Why do we measure time in hours and days?
Who decided that structure should guide our ways?

In the unknown, adventures unfold,
With laughter and questions, bright tales are told.
Wielding curiosity like a trusty sword,
We navigate life, ignoring the bored!

Curiosity at Twilight

Why do shadows stretch as the sun starts to sink?
Are they just trying to capture a wink?
If I chase the stars, will they run away?
Or do they just laugh at my clumsy ballet?

If dirt's what we tread, why is grass so green?
Is it the envy of leaves, or just part of the scene?
Why don't we see spiders when they do their dance?
Or are they just waiting for their chance?

Why does pizza taste better at midnight's door?
Is the hunger a trick or a culinary score?
If the fridge is a treasure, then what's the gold?
Leftovers wrapped in foil, a sight to behold!

When twilight descends, curiosity blooms,
In the oddest of questions, humor resumes.
So let's ask away as the evening takes flight,
For every "why" brings a giggle tonight!

Shadows of Seeking

In shadows cast by the flickering light,
I ponder the meaning, with all of my might.
The cat stares at me, is he judging my plans?
Or simply confused by my clumsy handstands?

With snacks on the table, I quest for the truth,
But the chips keep me busy, alas, I'm uncouth.
Do the answers even care if I crunch them aloud?
Or am I just lost in a snack-loving crowd?

Is the moon just a cheese wheel high in the sky?
While stars are just sprinkles, who knows what, oh why?
The dog barks a laugh, he thinks it's all grand,
But he really just wants to fetch something and stand!

As questions run wild in this whimsical chase,
I trip over thoughts that all seem out of place.
Yet laughter erupts as I learn not to brood,
For maybe the fun is in seeking the good.

Joy in the Questions

With a grin on my face, I ponder the day,
Are socks just for feet, or can they dance and play?
Can a spoon ever dream of being a fork?
I ask while I'm munching on salty and corked.

The fridge holds secrets, a treasure, it seems,
Are pickles the answer to all of my dreams?
The salad just giggles, all green and all bright,
It's laughing, I swear, in a veggie delight!

Oh, what if the clouds are just pillows of fluff?
Can laughter be bottled, or is that too tough?
The answers elude like a butterfly's flight,
But I'll chase them around till the morn turns to night.

In questions, I find a delightful parade,
With giggles and chuckles, and never dismayed.
The joy's in the query, not just in the quest,
For humor, it seems, keeps my heart feeling blessed.

The Language of Inquiry

What's the language of thought, is it spoken or mime?
Can questions be tasted like sweet lemon-lime?
As I sip on my soda, I ponder the flow,
Are answers just bubbles, they come and they go?

The goldfish just swims in a bowl full of dreams,
Does he know all the answers, or just how to scheme?
He flicks his tail boldly as I scratch my head,
Is he mocking my ponderings, or just want to spread?

Can a coat say it's cozy without wearing a hug?
Does the blanket feel warm while it's snug as a bug?
As I roll on the floor, and the laughter erupts,
I ask if it's funny when life interrupts.

In the circus of questions, I swing from the ropes,
With each silly query, my mind just elopes.
Who needs all the answers, when humor's the key?
In the dance of inquiry, I'll chuckle with glee!

A Tidal Wave of Thought

A tidal wave crashes, with thoughts in a whirl,
Do jellybeans giggle, or simply just twirl?
With a spoonful of sugar and dreams in my head,
I surf on the waves where my silly thoughts tread.

Can time take a break, or play hide and seek?
Is the clock really clever, or just a big freak?
I ask the goldfish, who swims with a grin,
What part of my chaos do I find my win?

Are the clouds soft as marshmallows, drifting up high?
Should I leap from my chair and just float in the sky?
The answers elude me like butterflies bright,
But the laughter I find makes it all feel so right.

In the splash of the questions, I twirl and I dive,
With joy in my heart, oh, I'm truly alive!
For in this great ocean where wonders collide,
It's the comedy of questions that I'll ever ride.

Threads of Inquiry

Why do socks vanish in the wash?
They slip away, they just can't stay.
Was it a sock party, a wild bash?
Or an escape plan? Who's to say?

When we ask why or how it's so,
Do the answers think they're real bright?
Will we find them, as we seek and go,
Or are they shy and hide at night?

Why does coffee spill and stain my shirt?
Is it a message or just bad aim?
Maybe it's laughing, or just a flirt,
Leaving me guessing, oh, what a game!

As we ponder and scratch our heads,
Do our thoughts trip on tangled vines?
In a chaser's chase, our worry spreads,
But confusion often wears the finest lines.

Beyond the Horizon of Knowing

What's on the other side of the moon?
Is it cheese? Or a park with a slide?
Do astronauts party on a balloon?
Questions stack up, can't let them hide.

When the fridge hums its nightly tune,
Is it complaining or just feeling shy?
Does it hold secrets, like a loony cartoon?
Seeking the truth, we sigh and pry.

Is time a matter, or a pesky thief?
Does it hold riddles more tight than a vault?
Can we steal moments, or is it just grief?
With each tick-tock, we can't help but halt.

When you ask a question, is it for fun?
Will you get answers or just see the clues?
Like a jester who dances but won't come undone,
In the circus of queries, we just can't lose.

Reflections on the Edge

If water could talk, what tales would it tell?
Of fishy adventures and splashes of fate?
Then why do we ponder the waves' gentle swell?
Maybe the sea just loves to create.

Do clouds have meetings to plan their rain?
Or do they drift, like a lazy thought?
Is thunder a joke or just nature's disdain?
All of these riddles, I'm caught in a knot.

What's hiding in shadows, where secrets reside?
Is it ghosts? Or just whispers of breeze?
With every doorway, I feel I've been lied,
As questions swirl like leaves in the trees.

Why do we search for sense in a jest?
When absurdities are all around us here?
In this funhouse mirror, we're put to the test,
Let's laugh at the riddles and not live in fear!

The Dance of Ambiguity

Is the cat really plotting our doom?
Or does it sleep, dreaming of fish?
In the grand scheme, do we all have room?
For questions like this, I make a wish.

When flowers bloom, do they know their song?
Do they dance with the sun, or just sway?
Are the bees buzzing, or are they wrong?
In this garden of doubt, who leads the play?

Why do we trip on thoughts we can't grasp?
Is it the universe pulling our leg?
Perhaps, in each query, we find a clasp,
Tying us tighter, like a life-sized peg.

In this waltz with the unknown, let's have some fun,
Float on the questions like leaves on the breeze,
For when we inquire, the jest has begun,
And clarity hides while laughter agrees.

The Poetry of Paradox

In the quiet of chaos, we wonder aloud,
Is a chicken a thinker? Or just part of the crowd?
Should socks match our mood, or is mismatched the goal?

We ponder such matters; they lighten the soul.

With ice cream for dinner, we laugh at the fate,
Is dessert for the brave, or for those who can't wait?
If gravity's real, then how do we float?
These silly debates make us ponder and gloat.

Echo Chamber of Queries

In a room full of mirrors, reflections abound,
Do they echo our thoughts, or just make a sound?
Do raccoons hold meetings to plan their big heist?
We question the logic, but who can say twice?

If I plant a fake tree, does it grow in my mind?
Can pizza be healthy, if just one slice is blind?
With riddles and laughter, we chase after sense,
Remember, dear friend, the nonsense is dense.

The Flicker of Doubt

In the flicker of light, do shadows have dreams?
Do wishes come true, or are they just beams?
When socks disappear, where do they prefer?
Do they travel the world, or just dream of the fur?

As we spin on this ball where logic takes naps,
We question our sanity, and giggle at cats.
If fish could speak, would they tell us the truth?
Or just blurt our secrets, and giggle in youth.

Dreams Drift Away

When dreams take a flight, do they fly with great style?
Or do they just wander, rest a while?
Are unicorns lazy, or just avoiding the grind?
With questions like these, who's losing their mind?

A fish in a pond thinks it's the king of the sea,
While turtles keep secrets, perhaps just from me.
With humor entwined, we search for the rhyme,
In the dance of absurdity, we're lost but in time.

Tapestry of the Unsure

In the morning I ask, toast or cereal?
Yet both seem to tempt with their appeal.
Should I jog or nap, the choices abound,
Confusion reigns, my thoughts spin around.

Is it time to wear socks with sandals so bold?
Or stick with the norm and just do what I'm told?
I ponder the colors of socks in my drawer,
While the coffee brews slowly, what else is in store?

With every email, my mind starts to race,
Reply or ignore, what's a polite pace?
Do I laugh at the jokes or just nod like a sage?
The questions keep coming, I'm caught in a cage.

So I scribble my thoughts on the back of an ice cream,
Maybe next week, I'll finally find my theme.
In this vast universe, questions abound,
Is ignorance bliss, or is that just a sound?

Unraveled Mysteries

Why did I enter this shop full of hats?
To try them on all, where's the harm in that?
Is this one too big, or too small, or too bright?
I stare in the mirror—am I wrong, am I right?

Should I buy a llama or a pet iguana?
My neighbors will talk, but they will love 'Rana'.
Is it weird to chat with my plants as I weep?
Or do they appreciate company, just don't sleep?

When I trip on the sidewalk, do I laugh, do I cry?
Will the squirrels take pity, or just scurry by?
Did I wear mismatched shoes? Oh what a surprise!
Are they judging my fashion or just rolling their eyes?

Questions are funny, they tickle and tease,
The more I ponder, the less I can please.
In a world full of riddles, I'll dance in the haze,
Unraveling sketches of my puzzly days.

The Quest for Clarity

Should I have pancakes or just settle for eggs?
The chef gives a wink, should I just eat some dregs?
Do I ask for the special, or stick to the norm?
With my stomach a-rumbling, it's hard to keep warm.

I search for my keys, where could they have flown?
Did I leave them at work or leave them at home?
Why did I open the fridge for a snack?
And now I'm just standing here, where was I at?

Will the sun ever shine, or rain on my parade?
I'm juggling these thoughts while I'm making my trade.
Is that a conundrum? Or just silly old fluff?
If the answers are out there, they're surely just tough.

I scribble down notes, like a detective of sorts,
To crack all the codes that nature reports.
With giggles I chase each uncertain delight,
As I ponder the cosmos, with questions in flight!

Between A Question and An Answer

What's the right greeting, a wave or a nod?
Do we shake or just smile, or is that too odd?
Is it awkward to stand in this line, all alone?
Or does small talk make strangers feel less like stone?

Why does my cat stare, with eyes full of tales?
Is she plotting world dominance, setting some trails?
Should I buy her a toy or just let her be free?
In her kingdom of chaos, she rules, can't you see?

When does a tantrum turn into a rant?
And if I shout loudly, will someone take a chance?
What if my pizza arrives with no cheese?
Will I still eat it, or mourn over my tease?

Questions tumble like laundry, they spiral around,
Each fabric a story, some lost, some found.
In the dance of confusion, let laughter be chief,
For the quest for the answers brings only some grief.

Whispers of the Unasked

Why is it always socks that flee?
Every dryer dance, a mystery.
Do they seek adventure, or a mate?
Maybe they're plotting to escape fate.

What's for dinner? A daily quiz.
Leftovers whisper, 'Please, not this!'
I swear the fridge has a sense of humor,
Every meal turns into a rumor.

Is there such a thing as too much cheese?
Or does it unlock the heart with ease?
I've lost count of my midnight snacks,
Here's to the truth that never lacks.

What's the point of counting sheep?
Do they wake us or make us weep?
Answers come wrapped in riddles tight,
Let's dance with questions into the night.

Shadows of Uncertainty

Why do pigeons always look so wise?
Perhaps they decode our clumsy lies.
They strut around like they own the place,
Maybe they're judging us, just a trace.

Why do cats knock things off the shelf?
Is it a sport or just for themselves?
Each crash could lead to a deep debate,
Is that a hobby or a cruel fate?

Does time travel really exist?
If so, why isn't my past more missed?
Should I chase it or just let it go?
Life's like a circus, a marvelous show.

Can plants hear when we softly speak?
Or do they plot while we lie awake?
Each leaf a listener, holding a grudge,
Sharing secrets that they won't budge.

The Pathway to Queries

Why do we trip on flat, clear ground?
Hurdles pop up where none are found.
Is the universe playing a jest?
Or are our toes just keen for unrest?

Who decided that carrots are good for sight?
Yet chips and cookies seem to take flight.
Do greens hold secrets, hidden from us,
While munching away at the food bus?

How do socks always find their pair?
Is there a sock gnome lurking down there?
Each laundry day, a new mystery waits,
As I wrestle with fate while the washing dominates.

Do we ever really know our thoughts?
Or are they like clothes that we just bought?
Each day's a fashion show, bright and bold,
Echoing stories yet to be told.

Beneath the Surface of Knowing

What's the deal with all these bees?
Buzzing about like they hold degrees.
Do they have jobs or just take flight,
Painting the world in sweet delight?

Why do we lose our keys each day?
Perhaps they're off on a grand display.
Hidden in pockets or under the bed,
Planning their escape while we dread.

Is the cookie jar a treasure chest?
Or a land of guilt we should invest?
Each bite a joy, each crumb a crime,
Yet we all sin just one more time.

Do shoes have feelings after a run?
Are they happy or do they just shun?
Each scuff a story, each crease a tale,
In this wild world, we all set sail.

Beyond the Horizon of Understanding

Why do socks just disappear,
Yet my laundry's always near?
The fridge seems to hold its secrets tight,
Where did I put that burger bite?

The cat stares with a knowing gaze,
While I puzzle over my own malaise.
Why's the toaster now on strike?
Did it just not like my bagel hike?

When did the remote become a ghost?
It's lost more often than I can boast.
Questions pile like dirty dishes,
Making sense, like quicksand, squishes.

Some say answers come in time,
But I'm still stuck on silly rhyme.
Maybe wisdom's just a slow reveal,
Or the universe loves a good comedic meal.

The Grid of Uncertainty

Life's like a game of chess, it seems,
Part strategy, part half-baked dreams.
I try to plan every single move,
Yet the board changes—what a groove!

Why do we worry what others think?
When all they do is at the bar drink.
I write my woes on a paper napkin,
While pondering why my sandwich is slackin'.

Questions dance like dust motes in the sun,
Twisting and twirly, just for fun.
Why does my phone need an update now?
I just want to browse, not take a bow!

In this grid, rules are seldom exact,
So I'll just improvise and leave no track.
Confusion reigns, but I'll grab a drink,
And toast to the thoughts that make us think!

Fragments of What-Could-Be

I plan a trip, a grand escape,
Then trip on shoes, oh what a scrape!
The map is lost, directions won't stick,
The GPS just laughs—what a trick!

Why does dinner need so much spice?
My tongue's now paying a hefty price.
Should I add more cheese, or just let it go?
Forecast calls for a cheesy snow!

Questions bubble like a pot on the stove,
While I wonder if I'll ever groove.
What if cake was a food group, you see?
Then dessert would be a daily decree!

In a world where chaos takes the lead,
I nibble on snacks, my only creed.
Fragments of wishes float like balloons,
What a delightful mess lifts my tunes!

The Journey of the Perplexed

Packed my bags for a journey bold,
But forgot the snacks—oh, what a hold!
Questions follow like a loyal friend,
Will I return? Or just pretend?

Why's the coffee cold? I brewed it twice,
Is my mug a portal to some device?
As I sip, thoughts swirl like the cream,
Perplexed by nature, lost in a dream.

Each step taken feels oh-so-quirky,
Like walking on eggshells made of jerky.
Why do ducks waddle and seem so wise?
They quack and laugh, while I analyze.

In this journey, confusion reigns supreme,
But I chuckle and let go—what a scheme!
For every enigma, there's a silly grin,
Guess I'll just embrace the chaos within!

Horizons of Inquiry

Why do socks vanish, oh where do they flee?
Does toast land buttered, or is it just me?
When I water the plants, do they aspire to roam?
And how do the cats know we're not home?

Where does the dust go when I finally clean?
Is it out living life, or just stuck in between?
Why do we park in a driveway yet drive in a park?
And who wrote the rules for the light in the dark?

Is the cake really better when it's made from a box?
Do fish ever ponder the thoughts of their flocks?
Why do we Google what we already know?
And who let the dogs out? We still don't know!

If I talk to my plants, am I truly insane?
Do trees gossip about the squirrels in vain?
Where do all the spare keys in life disappear?
And why do we search for what's already here?

Letters to Tomorrow

Dear tomorrow, do you have all the answers?
What's the secret, when the coffee's a disaster?
Why is it that kids grow so fast yet so slow?
And how do we know if our cake's a big show?

What really is 'normal'? Is it just a facade?
Can I barter with time, like a flea market god?
Do clouds ever think 'will we rain, or just float?'
And why does the car always seem to emote?

Tell me tomorrow, will my plants ever thrive?
Is it my watering skills, or they just connive?
Why is the remote always stuck in plain sight?
Does the fridge feel ashamed when I'm home late at night?

In letters I ponder the whims of the day,
Are hiccups just whispers from the universe's way?
Can dreams truly teach us what we must embrace?
Or is it just nonsense we conjure in space?

The Flickering Flame of Hope

Is optimism a candle, or just an odd spark?
What fuels all the wishes when daylight turns dark?
Do we truly need silence to think a grand thought?
Or can giggles and chuckles untangle what's taught?

Can hope take a selfie, or write us a song?
Is it friendly or feisty, or where does it belong?
What happens to wishes that float in the sky?
Do they trip on the stars, or just wave their goodbye?

When the fridge hums a tune, is it singing for joy?
Or just grumbling loudly, 'please fix that toy?'
In the seams of reality, where does nonsense dwell?
Is it wrapped up in stories we never could tell?

Can a daydream be squished under heavy stress?
Or do it bounce back, donning funny dress?
In that flickering flame, does laughter ignite?
Are we all just skits, on a stage of pure light?

Spectacles of Wonder

Where do I buy those glasses of insight?
That show me the world bathed in laughter and light?
Is the sky always blue, or is it just a tease?
And do the clouds plot mischief while dancing the breeze?

If curiosity's king, then why wear a crown?
Can I trade in my worries for a fun, silly frown?
Do puddles reflect dreams, or just raindrops in flight?
And are ants in a hurry, or just living their flight?

What's the point of a mitt, if no snow's ever near?
Is it all just a game, or our hearts live in cheer?
When I drink from the cup, is it coffee or mirth?
Or just two drops of giggles giving birth?

So many wonders disguise the mundane,
Like ducks in the park that just dance in the rain.
With spectacles in hand, let's ponder, and play,
For the world's a grand stage, and we're here for the fray!

www.ingramcontent.com/pod-product-compliance
Lightning Source LLC
Chambersburg PA
CBHW071821160426
43209CB00003B/159